instant Art
STORYTELLING

PARABLES AND MIRACLES

ILLUSTRATED BY
STEVE ENGLISH

**kevin
mayhew**

First published in 2003 in Great Britain by

KEVIN MAYHEW LTD
Buxhall, Stowmarket, Suffolk, IP14 3BW
E-mail: info@kevinmayhewltd.com

KINGSGATE PUBLISHING INC
1000 Pannell Street, Suite G, Columbia, MO 65201
E-mail: sales@kingsgatepublishing.com

9 8 7 6 5 4 3 2 1 0

ISBN 1 84417 074 8
Catalogue No 1396092

Cover design by Angela Selfe
Typesetting by Fiona Connell Finch

Printed in Great Britain

Contents

The paralysed man

Matthew 9:2-7; Mark 2:3-12; Luke 5:18-25

One day Jesus was preaching in a house and it was so crowded that no one else could get inside.

A1 The paralysed man   Jesus preaching in a crowded room

Some men came carrying a paralysed man on his mat but they could not get into the house because of the crowds.

A2 The paralysed man

Friends cannot get the man in

So they went up onto the roof and removed the tiles and dug through to make a hole.

A3 The paralysed man

Friends make a hole in roof

They then lowered the man through the roof and down at Jesus' feet.

A4 The paralysed man

They lower him in

Seeing their faith, Jesus turned to the man and told him his sins were forgiven. But teachers of the law who were there were thinking to themselves about what right Jesus had to forgive sins.

A5 The paralysed man

Jesus heals the man

Jesus knew what they were thinking and asked them which was easier, to forgive sins or to tell the man to get up and walk. To prove that he had the authority to forgive sins he told the man to get up, take his mat, and go home. He did so and everyone was amazed.

A6 The paralysed man

Man takes up his mat

Feeding the 5000

Matthew 14:15-21; Mark 6:35-44; Luke 9:12-17; John 6:5-13

People had followed Jesus to a lonely place. So he healed the sick and spoke to them about the Kingdom of God.

B1 Feeding the 5000

Jesus healing many people

As evening came the disciples asked Jesus to send the crowd away so that they could get something to eat. But Jesus asked his disciples to feed the people themselves.

B2 Feeding the 5000

Disciples complain that people are hungry

Andrew brought a boy to Jesus who had five loaves and two fish.

B3 Feeding the 5000

Boy with fish and loaves

Jesus asked the disciples to sit everyone down on the grass. Looking up to heaven he then broke the food and gave thanks for it.

B4 Feeding the 5000

Jesus gives thanks and breaks bread

He divided it up and gave it to the disciples to distribute. Everyone ate their fill and afterwards twelve baskets were collected of the remainder so that nothing was wasted.

B5 Feeding the 5000

People eat fill and remainder collected in baskets

Jairus' daughter

Matthew 9:18-25; Mark 5:22-42; Luke 8:41-56

A synagogue ruler called Jairus came to Jesus. He fell on his knees and asked him to come and heal his daughter who was dying.

C1 Jairus' daughter

Jairus goes to Jesus

On the way a woman who suffered from bleeding touched the hem of Jesus' cloak. Immediately the bleeding stopped and she was healed.

C2 Jairus' daughter

Woman touches coat in crowd

Jesus realised power had gone out of him and asked the crowd who had touched him. The woman came forward and told Jesus the truth. He told her that her faith had healed her and to go in peace.

C3 Jairus' daughter

Jesus heals woman

When Jesus entered Jairus' house he heard the flute players and the mourners making such a noise. He told them to go away because the girl was not dead but only asleep.

C4 Jairus' daughter

Jesus tells mourners to go

They all laughed at him.

C5 Jairus' daughter

They laugh at him

When the crowd had been put outside he took the girl by the hand and told her to get up. At once she stood up and her parents were amazed.

C6 Jairus' daughter

Jesus brings the daughter back to life

Calming the storm

Matthew 8:23-27; Mark 4:37-41; Luke 8:22-25

Jesus and his disciples were in a boat crossing the Sea of Galilee. Jesus was very tired and he fell asleep in the back of the boat.

D1 Calming the storm

Jesus and disciples cross Galilee

All of a sudden a great storm rose up on the sea and the waves swept over the boat.

D2 Calming the storm

Storm hits boat

The disciples were afraid and thought they were going to drown. They woke Jesus and asked him to save them.

D3 Calming the storm

Disciples wake Jesus

Jesus asked them why they were afraid and told them they had little faith. He got up and rebuked the wind and the waves.

D4 Calming the storm

Jesus calms storm

The sea went completely calm and the disciples were amazed that the wind and the waves had obeyed Jesus.

D5 Calming the storm

Disciples are afraid

The Good Samaritan

Luke 10:30-37

There was a man travelling from Jerusalem to Jericho.

E1 The Good Samaritan

Man walking on road

All of a sudden he was attacked by robbers who stole his belongings and stripped him of his clothes. They beat him up and left him half dead.

Set on by thieves

Soon a priest came along on the same road, but hurried by on the other side.

INSTANT ART FOR STORYTELLING – PARABLES & MIRACLES

E3 The Good Samaritan

Priest passes by

Then a Levite came, but he too hurried on his way without helping the man.

E4 The Good Samaritan

Levite passes by

Eventually a Samaritan came along and when he saw the man took pity on him. He bandaged his wounds and poured on oil and wine.

E5 The Good Samaritan

Samaritan helps

He then put him on his donkey and took him to an inn where he looked after him.

Takes man to inn

The next day he paid the inn keeper to continue caring for the man and promised that when he returned he would give him more money for any extra expenses.

E7 The Good Samaritan

Pays inn keeper to look after man

The lost son

Luke 15:11-32

There was a man who had two sons. The younger one wanted his share of the estate so the father divided his property between them.

F1 The lost son

Son wants his inheritance from father

Not long afterwards the younger son got together all his belongings and left home for a distant country. There he spent all his wealth on wild living.

F2 The lost son

Spends it on wild living

Soon there was a famine in that country and because he had no money he took on work feeding pigs. He was so hungry that he thought about eating what he was feeding to the pigs. When he came to his senses he decided to go back home and to beg his father for a job as one of his hired men.

F3 The lost son

Forced to tend pigs

While he was still a long way from home his father saw him and ran to him. He threw his arms around him and kissed him.

F4 The lost son

Father greets son

The son told his father how much he had sinned against him and how he was no longer worthy to be called his son. But the father got his servants to bring the best robe and sandals, and he put a ring on his finger and ordered the fattened calf to be killed for a feast. His son was dead but now was alive again. They all celebrated.

F5 The lost son   Kills fattened calf and puts ring on finger

The older son was angry that his younger brother, who had treated his father so badly, should have the fattened calf killed in his honour. He had never been given anything like that. But his father told his son that everything he had was his also and that they must be glad for his brother who had been lost but now was found.

F6 The lost son

Older son complains

The wise and foolish builders

Matthew 7:24-27; Luke 6:47-49

There was a man who built a house and he dug down deep and laid his foundation on rock.

G1 The wise and foolish builders   Wise man builds house on rock

Then the rain came down and the streams began to rise.

G2 The wise and foolish builders

Rain comes

The wind blew and beat against the house but the house stood firm.

G3 The wise and foolish builders

House stands firm

Another man also built a house, but he built his on sand.

G4 The wise and foolish builders

Foolish man builds house on sand

Then it started to rain and the streams began to rise.

G5 The wise and foolish builders

Rain comes

The wind blew and beat against the house and it fell with a great crash.

G6 The wise and foolish builders

House crashes

The lost coin

Luke 15:8-10

There was a woman who had ten silver coins.

H1 The lost coin

Woman has ten coins

However, one day she lost one of the coins.

So she lit a lamp and swept up through the whole house.

H3 The lost coin

Eventually she found the coin.

H4 The lost coin

She finds it

She called her friends and neighbours to celebrate with her because she had found her lost coin.

H5 The lost coin

Has a party with neighbours